92
LOPEZ   Guzmán, Lila

George Lopez

DUE DATE

FAMOUS LATINOS

George Lopez
Comedian and TV Star

Lila and Rick Guzmán

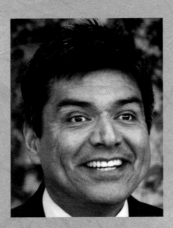

Enslow Elementary

an imprint of

Enslow Publishers, Inc.
40 Industrial Road
Box 398
Berkeley Heights, NJ 07922
USA

http://www.enslow.com

Series Adviser
Bárbara C. Cruz, Ed.D., Series Consultant
Professor, Social Science Education
University of South Florida

Series Literacy Consultant
Allan A. De Fina, Ph.D.
Past President of the New Jersey Reading Association
Professor, Department of Literacy Education
New Jersey City University

Note to Parents and Teachers: The *Famous Latinos* series supports National Council for the Social Studies (NCSS) curriculum standards. The Words to Know section introduces subject-specific vocabulary words.

This series was designed by Irasema Rivera, an award-winning Latina graphic designer.

Enslow Elementary, an imprint of Enslow Publishers, Inc.

Enslow Elementary® is a registered trademark of Enslow Publishers, Inc.

Copyright © 2006 by Enslow Publishers, Inc.

Library of Congress Cataloging-in-Publication Data
   Guzmán, Lila, 1952–
      George Lopez : comedian and TV star / Lila and Rick Guzmán.
      p. cm. — (Famous Latinos)
   Includes index.
   ISBN 0-7660-2644-2
   1. Lopez, George, 1961–   .—Juvenile literature. 2. Comedians—United States—
Biography—Juvenile literature. 3. Television actors and actresses—United States—
Biography—Juvenile literature. 4. Hispanic American comedians—United States—Biography—
Juvenile literature. 5. Hispanic American television actors and actresses—United States—
Biography—Juvenile literature. I. Guzmán, Rick. II. Title. III. Series.
   PN2287.L633G89 2005
   792.702'8092–dc22

                                                      2005031770

Printed in the United States of America

10 9 8 7 6 5 4 3 2 1

To Our Readers
We have done our best to make sure all Internet addresses in this book were active and appropriate when we went to press. However, the author and the publisher have no control over and assume no liability for the material available on those Internet sites or on other Web sites they may link to. Any comments or suggestions can be sent by e-mail to comments@enslow.com or to the address on the back cover.

Every effort has been made to locate all copyright holders of material used in this book. If any errors or omissions have occurred, corrections will be made in future editions of this book.

Illustration Credits: AP/Wide World, pp. 1, 4 (portrait), 14, 19, 20, 21, 22, 23, 24, 26, 27; Everett Collections, pp. 10, 16, 17, 28; Ted Faber, p. 7; Courtesy of George Lopez, pp. 4 (both childhood photos), 6, 8, 11, 12, 13.

Cover Illustrations: AP/Wide World.

✳ Contents ✳

1971

1978

George Lopez

1

A Blade of Grass

On February 21, 2004, George Lopez walked on stage to do his comedy act, called *Why You Crying?* People were excited to see him. They leaped to their feet and started to clap wildly. After the applause died down, George told jokes and stories for two hours. The people in the theater laughed and laughed.

Ever since he was eleven years old, George wanted to be a comedian. He always loved to make people laugh. George worked hard for many years, and his dream came true.

George Lopez was born on April 23, 1961, in Los Angeles, California. When he was two months old, his

George liked playing Little League baseball.

father left home. George never saw him again. George's family was Mexican American. He grew up speaking "Spanglish," a combination of Spanish and English.

George was an only child. All his friends had brothers and sisters. He was sad and lonely. One day, George was playing in the sandbox at school when a boy named Ernie Arellano joined him. George and Ernie became best friends. Growing up, they did everything together. They rode bikes, played, and watched television. Ernie was like a brother to him.

George's mother and his grandparents, Benita and Refugio Gutiérrez, were very poor. There was no money for birthday parties and presents. His family could not afford to buy toys or sports equipment.

So George had to make his own fun. He and Ernie learned how to play golf by hitting lemons that fell off a lemon tree in the backyard.

One bright spot in George's life was going to baseball games with his grandfather. They drank punch and ate homemade burritos while they watched the game. George loved baseball.

Going to Dodger Stadium with his grandfather was great fun for George.

A family picture from left: George with his grandmother and grandfather and his grandfather's father.

George had many hard times as a child. His mother was in and out of his life. When he was ten years old, his mother married and moved away for good. She left George with her mother and stepfather. George grew up with his grandparents in Mission Hills, California. His grandmother was tough and angry. She often yelled at him. "Why you crying?" she would demand.

One day, George saw a blade of grass growing in a crack in the concrete sidewalk. It seemed amazing. There was concrete everywhere, yet the grass still managed to grow. George's unhappy childhood was as hard as that concrete sidewalk. Yet George managed to grow. He said he was like that blade of grass.

❋ 2 ❋

Becoming a Comedian

On September 13, 1974, George watched a new television show called *Chico and the Man*. One of the stars of the show was Freddie Prinze. Freddie's mother was Puerto Rican, so he was Latino, like George.

Freddie Prinze was very funny. George could not stop laughing. Seeing that show changed George's life. He hung a picture of Freddie on his bedroom wall. George said to himself: "I can be a comic. I can do what Freddie is doing. I want to make people laugh."

Freddie Prinze was so funny on television!

On June 4, 1979, George went on stage for the first time. He was eighteen years old. It was a night he would never forget. He stood in front of an audience at a comedy club and told jokes. No one laughed. George felt terrible, but he did not give up. Instead, George and his friend Ernie worked for months writing a new comedy act. They tried to make the jokes funnier.

In high school, George was not a good student. He was always cracking jokes and causing trouble. He failed English and had to take it over in summer school. On August 6, 1979, he finally got his high school diploma. He was the first person in his family to graduate from high school.

Over the next few years, George had several different jobs. He did not like any of them. In 1987, when he was twenty-six, he decided to become a full-time comedian. George traveled from club to club doing his comedy act. Sometimes people laughed at his jokes, and sometimes they did not.

George appeared sixteen times on *The Arsenio Hall Show*, a popular television show. He performed in lots of clubs. But half the seats in the clubs were empty. He was feeling bad. Should he give up?

George, left, with his best friend, Ernie, in the 1980s.

George started telling jokes in comedy clubs.

In May 1989, George met Ann Serrano, a Cuban-American woman who was an actress and casting director, the person who chooses actors for a show. She saw his act and believed he would become a star someday. She told him to keep trying.

George and Ann fell in love. They married on September 18, 1993. Three years later, their daughter, Mayan, was born.

During the 1990s, George performed in many comedy clubs. He was growing more popular, and the clubs were filling up. He had some small parts in movies and television shows. He was in a movie called *Bread and Roses*. It was shown at an important movie festival in Cannes (KAN), France. He turned down roles that showed Latinos as drug dealers or gang members.

Ann and George on their wedding day.

In 2000 George worked for a while as the host of a radio show. He was the first Latino host who spoke English, not Spanish, on a morning radio show in Los Angeles. He was also doing his comedy act. George knew he was a good comic, but he wanted to be *great*.

Then, one night, it happened. A famous actress named Sandra Bullock came to the comedy club to see George perform. George did not know it, but he was about to become a big star.

The actress Sandra Bullock, left, changed George's life.

3

The George Lopez Show

Sandra Bullock wanted to create a television show with Latinos as the main characters. The last Latino comedy on television was called *Trial and Error* and ran for only two weeks in 1988. She said this was not right. People should see more Latinos on television.

Then Sandra saw George perform his comedy act. His stories and jokes about his childhood and his family were so funny. Sandra thought that George's life would make a great television show. "We have to do it!" she told him.

George's television show uses many parts of his real life. The main character is named George.

The cast of *The George Lopez Show* in 2002.

He works in an airplane parts factory. His wife is Cuban-American, just like the real Ann Lopez. His best friend, Ernie, is based on Ernie Arellano. The mother on *The George Lopez Show* is named Benny. Her character is based on George's grandmother Benita.

ABC-TV liked the idea of presenting a show about a Latino family. *The George Lopez Show* started on March 27, 2002. Twelve million people watched the show. George's television family faces the same kinds of problems as any other family. The show is not just for Latinos. George was very happy to hear that everybody, not just Latinos, enjoyed his show.

The George Lopez Show quickly became a hit. It was the first successful Latino comedy since *Chico and the Man*. For the first time in his life, George felt like a big success.

Sometimes Sandra plays Accident Amy, a clumsy factory worker.

4

Helping Others

Things started moving very fast in George's life. His show won a Parents Television award. He did his comedy act for President George W. Bush. He got an important part in the movie *Real Women Have Curves* (2002). It is about a Mexican-American girl who wants to go to college. George plays the teacher who helps her reach her dream.

When George was invited to play in a special golf tournament, he was thrilled. Golf is his favorite sport. Some of the golfers were professionals, which means that playing golf is their job. The others, like George, were amateurs. They play golf for fun, as a hobby. Of all the amateur players, George had the best score.

George loves playing golf.

George was happy that his life was going so well. He wanted to share his success. He began using some of his time and his money to help others. He has become well known for all he does for people in need. He speaks out against street gangs and violence. He raises money for earthquake victims. He and Ann started their own charity to give money for education in the arts. George has won many awards as an actor and a comedian. He has been honored for being a generous, caring person.

For George, a special moment in his life came in March 2004. The cable television network TV Land decided to honor Freddie Prinze, who had

George rode a horse onto the stage at the Latin Grammy Awards show in 2004.

died many years earlier. He was still George's favorite star, and George was asked to present the award. Freddie's son, who is also named Freddie Prinze, thanked George for the award.

George's book about his life, *Why You Crying?*, was published in 2004. Many readers were interested to learn more about George, and the book was a big success. His CD *Team Leader* was one of the best

George holds the book about his life: *Why You Crying?*

comedy albums of 2004. It was nominated for a Grammy Award for Best Comedy Album.

George starred in the 2005 movie *The Adventures of Shark Boy & Lava Girl in 3-D*. George played a few different characters in this story of a boy and his two imaginary friends with superpowers.

George was busy and successful as an actor and comedian. Then he got some bad news. There was a problem with his kidneys. If he did not get a healthy kidney, he could die. George's wife, Ann, said she wanted to give George one of her kidneys. On April 19, 2005, George and Ann went into the hospital. Doctors operated on both of them. Ann said that giving George a kidney was an easy choice because she loved him and wanted him to be healthy.

The operation was a surprise to many people. They did not know that George had been ill for several years. Three weeks later, George was well enough to play golf. He and Ann were very happy. They became the spokespeople for the National Kidney Foundation. George and Ann are speaking out to teach more people about kidney disease.

George, Ann, and their daughter, Mayan, went to see
The Adventures of Sharkboy and Lavagirl in 3-D.

It was a happy day for George and Freddie Prinze Jr. when Freddie's father was honored with a star on the Hollywood Walk of Fame.

✳ 5 ✳

George and His Hero

When George was a teenager, he put a picture of his hero, Freddie Prinze, on the wall of his bedroom. Today, that picture hangs in George's television office. "The first time I saw him," George said, "I wanted to be like him. He was so young and cool and Latino and everybody loved him."

Having a star on the Hollywood Walk of Fame is a big honor. George thought Freddie should have this honor. George told other people his idea, and he worked hard to make it happen. In December 2005, Freddie got a star.

George on the set of his television show.

When George was a teenager watching *Chico and the Man*, he never imagined that one day he would become good friends with Freddie's son. Freddie Prinze had inspired George to become a comedian. Years later, in 2006, George helped Freddie Prinze Jr. start a television show, *Freddie*. George was glad to give Freddie Jr. advice and suggestions. Sometimes George appeared as a guest on *Freddie*.

The George Lopez Show reached one hundred episodes in 2006. George received a big honor: He got a star on the Hollywood Walk of Fame.

When George was a little boy he wanted to be someone important. Today, George is a famous comedian and actor who shares his time and money to help others. He tells people, "Dream big dreams." He believes that dreams come true every day. "I am living proof!" he says.

In 2006, George earned his own Hollywood star, too.

George hopes his success will be a spark for other people to follow their dreams, too.

✳ Timeline ✳

1961 George Lopez is born in Los Angeles on April 23.

1971 His mother moves away and leaves George with his grandparents.

1974 George sees Freddie Prinze on television and decides to become a comedian.

1979 Graduates from San Fernando Valley High School.

1979 Performs for the first time as a comedian, on June 4.

1993 Marries Ann Serrano on September 18.

1996 Daughter, Mayan, is born.

2002 *The George Lopez Show* begins on ABC-TV on March 27.

2005 Ann gives George a kidney. They become spokespeople for the National Kidney Foundation.

2006 George gets a star on the Hollywood Walk of Fame.

☀ Words to Know ☀

burrito—A popular Mexican food. A round flat bread, called a tortilla, with fillings like beans and cheese.

charity—A fund of money that is used to help needy people.

comedian—Someone who tells jokes to make people laugh.

comedy club—A place where comedians perform.

diploma—A paper stating that a person has finished school.

factory—A place where things are made. Cars are made in a car factory.

inspire—To be the reason someone wants to do something.

kidney—An important part of people's bodies. People are born with two kidneys, but they can live with one.

Spanglish—A mix of Spanish and English, such as, "I need to buy some limones."

tournament—A contest.

☀ Learn More ☀

Articles

Maria Elena Fernandez, "They're Linked in Spirit and in Schedule," *Los Angeles Times*, October 17, 2005.

James Poniewozik, "George Lopez: The Prime-Time Funny Man." *Time*, August 13, 2005.

"The 25 Most Influential Hispanics in America," *Time*, August 22, 2005.

Internet Addresses

George's Web site
<http://www.georgelopez.com>

Video clips and photographs
<http://www.georgelopez.com/media/media.html>

The Web site for George's television show
<http://abc.go.com/primetime/georgelopez/en/index.html>

✦ Index ✦